Poems from the heart

Book two

By Matthew R Brackley

A personal,intimate journey of poetry
encompassing love.
Full of emotion,thought and most of all......
you

ISBN978-1-291-45098-9

In a field of painted flowers
I claimed as my own
I stood
Inside of you

Index

On the sunlight sea
Touching you
Sea of cosmos
Winter walk
Moons and stars
In our room
Sweet lovings
On a golden sea
I fell for you
Golden heart
This soft glowing
The colours of the night
My blue world
About a girl
That single tear
Satellite
This mystical you
The colours of my heart
In a tranquil place
Set in you
The gift of giving part I
The gift of giving part II

For the heart is a sea,
flowing for you and me
The gentle roar.......
Sweet lovings
The love to pour
Sweet lovings on to the shore

Inside of you

In a field of painted flowers
I claimed as my own
I stood
Inside of you

In a heart
Filled to bursting
A sky filled with wonder
I sensed a hidden spring

You cannot hold
What I love about you
In a field of painted flowers
To your self
A sky filled with wonder
Coloured blue

Inside of you
I stood
I claimed as my own
In a field of painted flowers

Wild flower

Like a wild flower
I watched you grow
Budding
Blooming
Wanting you more

Your sweet perfume
Lingered on me
I lie awake
Remembering
Vividly

Like a wild flower
You swayed in the wind
You could not break
Only in my heart
I watched you
Wanting you more

The taste of you
Sweet honey
From a wild flower
I loved you too

Set in you

I saw the perfect jewel
Set in you
Such exquisiteness
In something
Precious and blue

Such lustrous fire
Set in you
The perfect jewel
How I wanted to touch
Everything too

I can see
The lustrous blue
That shone
Deep in your heart
So completely

Blue
The colour of sky
At twilight
Set in you
Exquisite
It's colour
Touched my heart

Precious and blue
In something
Such exquisiteness
Set in you
I saw the perfect jewel

In a swirl of stars

In a swirl of stars
I found you
Glitterbright
You lit up, an entire night

Poetry cannot say
Poetry cannot speak
The colours that I saw
In you
In the milky way

My heart
In a swirl of stars
To find you
In a night
Of deepest blue

I followed you
Glittering bright
For, in the darkest night
In a swirl of stars
I loved you too

Beneath a Western Sky

A Queens' jewelled hand
Lifted slowly,
pointed to the Western land

For, in the West
Stars were seen
Precious things
Hidden
Waiting to be found
In the forests of richest green

A star
Beneath a Western sky
A journey
With you
Deep in to the night

A Queens' jewelled hand
Lifted slowly
To a Western land
Where so many stars
Waiting to be found

Stars for you and I
To be found
Beneath a Western sky

The journey with you
To find this precious thing
Of a star...
Beneath a Western sky
Colour too

So many nights to pass
For, in a Western sky
You and I,
Will find a star
Waiting to be seen
In the forest of richest green

To the edge of night
You found..
What you were looking for..
In the west
Under starlight

Hand in hand
Walking through
Western land
I followed a star...
Found in a Western land
That star....
Was you

In the beauty of my youth

In the beauty of my youth
Such boundless energies
Love takes on a special meaning
Colours are brighter
All the senses magnified
Heightened dreaming

For, I dreamed of you
From a time long ago
When we were in love
Such intenseness
I felt it too

In the beauty of my youth
I looked back,
and in no time too
Saw you standing there
My heart squeezed
Such soft skin to touch
In what I dreamed of you

For, I dreamed of you
Time after time
I wanted you to know
That I loved you too
In the beauty of my youth....
I let you go

Glowing bright

I loved you
For, all the travelling
All you have seen
We saw together
In forests of richest green

I couldn't think of anything better
Than being with you tonight
All I wanted
Was here
Glowing bright

With eyes perfect and blue
I got lost...
In the power of you

I went in circles
Lost
Without you
What is a sea,
Without a sky
This is what it means to me

I wanted you to know
How bright
Your star shone
How far you have travelled
Now you have gone

All of you

So hard,you fell
I could never pick up
All the pieces
To make you whole
I gathered all
That was left
Blew softly
and kissed
Each piece
As though it were your soul
I cannot put it all
Back
I can, but try
I could never stop
Your fall
All the pieces too
That I found
What I gathered
Kissed
To make whole
All of you

To my first love

To my first love
I look back to those times
With wonder and delight
The delicate and gentle exploration
Of our bodies and minds
That reached new heights

Where can we begin?
For ten thousand miles of sea
Are in between
All that I know
Is what lies in my heart
Is not a sin

I want to see you again
Hold you, so very tight
Take away the pain
Never let you go

To my only love
I carry in my heart
Everyday
A picture of you
It has always been there
Where it always lay

One day...
It can be
That you and I
Are together
Both, free

Moondust

I followed a trail
At last light
Of Moondust
Until I found you
Glowing softly
In my night

A silver thread
To find
Of Moondust
That you left for me
In my night

When the sun, set
In pinks and reds
A moon rose
So did you
In my night

The softest light
Of Moondust
Carried my heart
So very far
In my night

A rising moon
Of palest silver
Of soft light
I thought of you
In my night

Be still,my love

Be still,
my love...
You cannot run
This unravelling...
Is now done

Be still,
my love...
I found you
In forests of richest green
Picking wild flowers of blue

Be still,
my love...
Come to the fire
In a deepening night
Watch the stars above

Be still,
my love...
The heart quickening
Under starlight
Stay with me till morning

Be still,
my love...
No more running
Such beauty and strength
I have found wanting

Be still,
my love...
For, now you know
A quickening heart
A soft glow

Be still,
my love...
In a dawn sky
Filled with colour
Is a place for you and I

Be still,
my love...
You cannot run
This travelling...
Is now done

That beauty lies within

So many doors
So many beautiful rooms
To explore
I need to find out more

I have only been
In the smallest part
Of the rooms and doors
That lie unseen
Deep in your heart

Can a magician find
The keys?
To the locks,
to the rooms,
of your mind?

One by one
To reveal
All of you
All of me
In a way
Only magic can see

That such beauty
Lies within
Behind a door
You cannot resist
I must open
The heart
To see all of you

I do not have a key
All I have...
Is the love in me
The willingness to open
The doors
Of you
Of me...

I have started the journey
To see the rooms and doors
That lie
Deep in your heart
To be discovered
By me...

For a girl

For a girl...
Whose heart
Can soar
Like a gull

I caught you
Upon wind
Soft and light
As you flew
In to the sun,bright

The silver wings
That you wore
The beauty...
My heart...
Tore

For,you must fly
In never ending light
One day...
I will climb up
and join you
In flight

For a girl...
That will always fly
Let her love unfurl
In perfect blue sky

I dreamed of you

I dreamed of you
On a winter night
That one day
Under a Heartstone Moon
We would meet
Soon
That it would be right

I dreamed of you
Of times past
Wished you were here too
Love to last

I dreamed of you
Close to me
The rise and fall of your chest
On a winter night
Is all I want to see

I dreamed of you
In a Heartstone summer
Your eyes, the colour of sky
Hand in hand
Running through
Forest and meadows too

I dreamed of you
You cannot stop
The emotional tide
That one day
I will be here

A heart, full of stars

I looked down
Upon your face
Wreathed in starlight
A heart...
Filled with delight

I wanted you to see
All that I am
In you
All that can be

I felt a star
In me
All that I am
All that you could see
Is for you.......

I looked down
Upon your face
Wreathed in starlight
A heart...
Filled with delight
Filled with stars

Mystic moon

shadows can cross
In a heart beat
Mystic moon
Deepening heat

Colours of shadow night
In your heart
Mystic moon
Mystic night

I held it there
In my heart
On the tip of my tongue
It was always there
Mystic moon

What I need
I need from you
Mystic moon
Shadows too

What are you going to do?
What I need...
Mystic moon
Shadows fall
I want you too

Mysterious night
Mystic moonlight
The fall of shadows
Nobody knows

In your heart
Lies a mystic moon
Your deep shadow light
To fall...
Across my night

To caress
Slowly across
Hidden depths
Fragrance to seep
A tongue
Piercing you deep

In the heat of the night
The heat of you
Mystic moon
Mystic night
Coming too

Did I do it right?

I winged my way.....
Through the night
When you opened your heart....
Opening the vulnerable you....
Exposed too
I saw nothing, but light

The love opens too....
Did I do it right?
Winging my way through the night
When I offer all....
Will she take it all?
Will I fall?

This is how I feel
The heart ,so full
Full for you....
What can I do?
but love you

Did I do it right?
I lie with you....
All through the night....
The love to spill,
my heart,
beginning to fill,
fill with light

To breathe you in....
The smell of your hair,
takes me there
How long is the night?
How long can I stay?

How long can I bear?
I want you too....
Did I do it right?

Mysteries of the heart

Shadows, flew
across my heart
Dark too

Such dark beauty
Such mystery
Shadows too,
in the heart

Amidst the shadows
A light grew
A spark...
A rose...
That was me

Spilling out
Petals falling
Colour calling,
I heard it shout

Mysteries of the heart
Such dark beauty,
becoming light

The smokiness within
The battle of light
The battle of dark
A curious whim
A curious spark

Light and shadows,
flew across my heart
Such beautiful things
Cannot rest in the
mysteries of the heart

On the Sunlight Sea

This love, magically so
Makes us free,
together,
golden glow,
on the sunlight sea

This energy I feel,
as I take the wheel
I now know
what is means, to be free,
for sunlight sea,
makes it so

This light air
on the sunlight sea
blows so fair
for you and me

A sea of azure,
in golden light
a lovers' touch,
love so pure
Our delight

This brilliant white sail
carries you and I
for our love cannot fail
on this golden trail

This magical sea,
so blue
Sailing with you,
is everything to me

On the sunlight sea,
everything comes true,
especially for you and me
All our dreams,
such delicate golden streams,
are what makes us free

On the sunlight sea
Where our love can be
This golden place,
upon deep blue
The love,....I see in your face
can only be true,
on the sunlight sea

This golden light
on a sea so bright
A sea so blue,
all my dreams'
in delicate golden streams
have come true

My love for you
on a sea of blue
is what is meant to be
on the sunlight sea

Touching You

In my dream....
I saw you there
Playing a field .
With me
In a land from nowhere

The flowers....
Flowed free....
Colour rippling....
In the wind
That blew....
For you and me

Running through....
Hand in hand....
This time to last....
The colour passed
I loved you too....

You gave to me
All that meant....
For me to see.....

The wind blew
Looking back at the sky
My heart...
To fly....
Touching you

In my dreams....
It became so real
You and me
Running through a field....
with colours , you can feel
colours you could see

If love was a colour
It would have glowed for you
Bright too....
Summer sky,
for you and I

In a field, with you
Looking back at a sky
With clouds rolling by....
Touching you

In a land from nowhere....
Colours, running free
I saw you there,
touching you
Wind off the sea....
Running with me....
Loving you

Sea of Cosmos

This bright blue sky,
reminds me of you.
I lie back in the field
of cosmos
to you.................
I yield

This meadow,
this cosmos,
Is my love so
For, beauty here
and beauty there,
Cosmos everywhere

This cosmos field
This bright blue sky
To you,
I yield

To lie back in the field,
in the warmth of the sun
Staring up,
to bright blue sky
This I yield
My heart to fly

Your cosmos flower,
chose me..........
In this colour sea
In the colour field
To you............
I yield
Your colour I see

Bright blue sky,
Pretty flowers sigh
Cosmos field,
to you
I yield
For here I lie

This soft wind,
blowing through me
This is what happened,
your cosmos flower,
in this field,
leant towards,
the inner me

This cosmos field
belongs to you and I
This cosmic colour sea,
dreamily sigh
We both yield,
under bright blue sky

Lying back in a cosmos sea
Looking up to bright blue sky
Soft wind blowing through,
this colour sea,
and you are with me too
I dreamily sigh

My cosmic colour sea............
where you are meant to be
it is you....
that I have taken there,
lying back, enjoying cosmic air
You .....
Yielded too

Winter Walk

Crackle of frost underfoot
This snow covered wood
Where I met you...........
for the first time

Clouds of breathy air,
your cloak of deep blue,
you made me stop and stare

For, among the holly,
we both were looking for the same thing
This cold pale sky,
with no hint of spring

Your first look,
took my breath away
Your shy smile,
melted me
The sun shone.........
On that day.......

Woods of evergreen,
dusted with snow
This walk..........
with you
Inner glow

This walk...........,
with you,
through snow
My heart,

Your hand,
warmed by mine
Your shy glance
How those blue eyes...
did dance!

This love did flow,
on this walk,
on fresh fallen snow
So white and clear,
surrounded by trees of green

Woods of evergreen,
fresh fallen snow
Where our love can be seen
footprints.......
side by side,
long ago

Where I first met you,
on that winters day,
among the holly and snow
You had far to go,
now together
Our way
seems so short so

Moons and Stars

Moons and stars
In a world
Belonging to you

I took a ride
With you
In a world
That you and I could hide

Moons and stars
That's how it can be
You and I
In a world
We made free

I took a ride
A cosmic glide
With you
Far
In a world
In a star

Moons and stars
That's the way
It ought to be
The way it ought to stay
In a world
Belonging to you and I

I took a ride
With you
In a heartbeat
A cosmic glide
A stars' heart

Moons and stars
In worlds
Belonging to you and I
I found you
You found me
In worlds
That ought to be

I took a ride
With you
A cosmic glide
In a sky
In a world
Made free
For you and I

Moons and stars
In a world
With you
Cosmic glide
So very far
Taking me too

I took a ride
Felt your warmth
In a sky
In a world
That ought to be
Always with you

In our Room

Burgundy drapes fall
From the window
This fireplace
The embers glow

Muted light
Reflecting
Panelled wood
Soft glowing

Crackle of wood
Flickering firelight
In our room
Our delight

Great Forest Tapestries
Of leaf and bark
Adorn the wall
Our forest
Our trees

In our room
Filled with books and firelight
The snow outside
Still falling
Soft scent of you
My heart,
calling

The soft hue
Of Tiffany lamps
Rugs from Persia
Being with you

In our room too
Billowing clouds
Tall ships sail
Of seas green and blue

Upon the hearth
The dogs lay
Snoring softly in firelight
They enjoyed the walk today

In our room
Flickering firelight
Illuminating the gloom
Snow outside
Soft and white

On a Golden sea

The colours....
Took me away....
From me....

The golden light...
Touched me
Touched you too...
On a golden sea

On the edge of light
looking down....
In to the night

You crossed a golden sea...
Just to be with me
I can understand....
How you left it all....
Leaving the bland
Just to be with me

A sail....
So far away
On a horizon of deepest blue
Coming to you.....
To take....
The inner you.....
Setting it free...
On a golden sea

The colours
Held me in sway...
Took me away
Let me go...
On a golden sea

I do not know....
What I search for
I will find it...
On a golden sea

A golden sea....
Where you found me
Searching...
For the inner you
To set it free

A horizon of deepest blue....
What it meant to you...
What it meant for me...
On a golden sea...
Standing on the edge of light
Looking in to the night

The colours, true
Set me free
On a golden sea
Took me to you

I fell for you

I fell for you........
The feathers fell too.....
Into the deep,
the deep of you

The feathers rained down,
golden bright
Lifted your frown.........
You came into the light

All things have a purpose......
You chose me....
In ways I never knew
This, I could see........
I could see in you

I fell........
In to the deep,
The deep of you
Feathers falling through
Feathers falling
Heart calling

Golden Heart

I searched for days.........
In the places dear to my heart
Some things can never be found,
when you are in a daze

If you look deep........
The thoughts and feelings you can reap
You can but try..........
To find the place........
Dear to you,
if you look deep and true

Such things,
so small to find
All of them ,in your mind
All have meanings

I searched for that glowing,
that people have inside
That knowing.........
they cannot hide

The colour is there,
like a piercing dart
a colour so rare............
The golden heart

A golden heart,
wreathed in love
A place dear to me
What I found,

what you can see
What you can see in me
Love can be.......
If you let it be found

This soft glowing

This soft glowing light....
I see in your eyes
My heart reflecting
You detecting.........
My plight

It is true.....
What they say
The eyes hold everything
The things you hold true
The heart play.......
The things the heart will do

The battle internal
The battle for the heart........
Eternal
The eyes hold the key..........
The key to you and me

This soft glowing
Pulling me........
Pulling me to you
Love flowing
The eyes have it too........

The flame,
needs a spark............
The day you came
The day I left the dark

This soft glowing.........
Reflected in eyes knowing
Spark to a flame.........
The day you came

The colours of the night

A sunset.....
Gold and red
Washed its' colours over you,
as we lie upon our bed

As thoughts spill.........
Like the colour
Bronze and gold
It is you I fill........
It is you I hold

Deepening red........
Upon our bed
Evening sky.......
Brings you to me,
for here we lie
You and I
Colours to spill
Colours to fill

Colours gold and red
Fading away
instead....
Our night of play........
At the end of the day

As you lie upon our bed........
The sky.........
Soft pink and blue
Here I lie with you.........
Thoughts read

Your love ....
Washed its' colours over me
Your sunset...........
Soft and pink........
Given free..........
As I give to you........
The deepening colour hue

Deepening purple and blue
Covered me...........
Covered you............
The covered night sky
Deepening delight............
For you and I

The night sky..........
Covered you and I
The colours of the heart.....
the colours of the night.....
Made you sigh.....

My blue world

My blue feathers support me
in this land of golden light,
for I drift down slowly to sea of blue

In my talons I hold a blue stone
blue fire,
tumbling light

For this blue stone holds my love,
I wheel and turn,
in puffs of wind,
the stone begins to burn

Heat of love sparking through,
blue of light too

I look for my soul mate,
she is near,
I sense it

My love,
of feathered gold
is close by,
for I cannot break the tie,
that we hold

Gold and blue
shines through
She rises to meet me,
from the sun,
golden sun

Golden heart
Going for the fire of blue,
sparking through

Gold joins blue,
colours mixed through.
Blue fire,golden hue

Two are as one,
blaze of golden blue light
Blue of sea and land,
gold of sun,
gold of sand

Golden hue,
and sapphire blue,
unfurled
in this blue world

Blue world
of sea and land,
gold world of
sun and sand

Release my blue stone of fire,
agony of desire.
Encompassing feathered gold
of which I never tire.
This blue sapphire
I hold tight and true,
sparks only for you

About a girl

Hair, so soft....
Hair to curl....
about a girl....

So much to see....
Beauty of her skin....
Breathe it all in....
The love....
coming free........

She gave.....
All of it to me
I yielded too.....
Gave all,true

Something has to give way......
This was me....
There you lay
I took you
My love to unfurl
All.....
About a girl
You see......

Skin ,so soft....
Beauty too....
Giving true....
About a girl....
Loving me

That single tear.....

Falling down your cheek
Holding back........
You don't want to let it go
You don't want to let it show

The tears must flow.......
This is good to know.......
Not all tears are bad
Not all tears are sad

The tears that flow
The tears to help you know

That single tear........
That you show
Wetness to feel.........
This I know..........
You are here

That single tear.........
Did more for me.......
More than you know.......
I am here

That single tear..........
What you can show
What you can see...........
You did for me........
I am here

That single tear.........
For me..........
Captured me completely
I am here

That single tear.........
That I kissed.........
I am here
What you missed

That single tear............
To heal
All that I feel..........
I am here

That single tear..........
Fell for me........
As I fell for you
I am here

This Mystical You

This mystical you
knows my every thought
This slender silver thread
that connects me to you
These feelings read
These feelings caught

This mystical you
What you do.........
to my soul
Opening up the power
like a budding flower

Instinctively knowing
The mystical you,
keeps it all flowing,
in to my deepest place,
unlocking the heart case,
filling it too

Slender silver thread
winds its way through,
the mystical you,
from heart to head
Flowing too

What you do,
petals unfold,
colours they hold
This mystical you
These thoughts foretold

My deepest place,
my opened heart case
Delicate silver thread
My thoughts read,
by mystical you

The colours of my heart

The colours of a sunset
Ran through my heart
Orange, gold and red

Shades of indigo
Became a midnight blue
The glorious night
The moon glow

Moonbeams
Shaped white clouds,
in to silver streams

The colours of the night
Ran through my heart
Silver and midnight blue

A blush in the east
As stars fade
Different colours returned
The shades of the heart
These things I learned

In a tranquil place

In a tranquil place
Known only to you
I could see the wind
Rustle through the trees
Rippling through
Like a green sea
Coming to me

A pleasant wind blew
Fresh and full
Carried the scent of you

Your hair, so soft
Spilled over,
on a pillow of blue
All I want...
Is you...

I touched your breast
Traced the outline,
of a nipple
Needing me
All I want...
Is you...

Delicious wetness
To feel...
Upon my fingers
Upon my tongue
All I want...
Is you...

I covered you
Felt my way inside..
Delicious wetness
Upon me
All I want...
Is you...

Such sweet release
Internal fire
Your body
My desire
All I want...
Is you...

In a tranquil place
Known only to you
I could see the wind
Rustle through the trees
Rippling through
Like a green sea
Coming to me

Set in You

I saw the perfect jewel
Set in you
Such exquisiteness
In something
Precious and blue

Such lustrous fire
Set in you
The perfect jewel
How I wanted to touch
Everything too

I can see
The lustrous blue
That shone
Deep in your heart
So completely

Blue
The colour of sky
At twilight
Set in you
Exquisite
It's colour
Touched my heart

Precious and blue
In something
Such exquisiteness
Set in you
I saw the perfect jewel

The Gift of Giving Part I

The giving is a gift.........
that few have,
that few know
The gift of giving so

So many people in this world.........
If they all gave......
How many people,
could they save?

The smallest act of giving,
can reach deep
New ways of living..........
Take a faith leap

The living gift
The loving gift
The healing rift

With two hands
I give to you
All I have......
All in me........
Feel me too

Feel me too.........
The gift.........
The gift of you

The Gift of Giving part II

Feel me too...........
The gift.............
The gift of you

To take on this loving light
It is true.............
That the gift,
is pure gold
That shines in darkened night
This gift from you to me

When two givers meet...........
Such richness explored
Internal light.......
Giving sweet........
This love poured

The gift,open to all
May it be..........
Only some...........
Recognize its' call
Only some can see
Only few come

For the gift you gave to me....
Felt in so many ways
The gift of giving,
is one my heart plays

My heart plays
So many things
So many ways
Yet it sings

To give..........
so many loving lights
To live.........
So many new heights

Only the few
Feel in so many ways
Those who give it too
The way the heart plays

The gift you gave to me
The gift of giving so
I feel so many ways
I know in so many heart plays
The richest gift you see
The richest gift I know

Post script

I have started the journey
To see the rooms and doors
That lie
Deep in your heart
To be discovered
By me...

Website

http://aquilamoondust.wix.com/red-sky

Other titles by Author

Poems from the heart
Poems from the heart book 2
A beautiful sky ,so red
Beneath a Western sky
My colour cosmic sea
Beautiful blue world
The wings of the heart
The Sea and the Sky
A river of stars
The narrow squeak show!
In War and in Battle
The poetry of flowers
Faerie Magick Midnight!
Heart of a storm
In the Moons' reflection
Castle Heartstone book 1
Castle Heartstone book 2
Castle Heartstone book 3
Aquila and Moondust

Yellow Moon Sea
A Heartstone Sky
Poems for children
Strange fish and other stories
The Forest Queen
In the Minds' Eye
The Star Tree
The Book of Stars
The Gift Wish
The love of all things
The Magic of the Trees
Golden Heart
Songs of Water
The Place of the Rising Moon
In the light,beautiful things
The Turrets of Sky
Dragonflies and Hearts
Sails at sunset

www.ingramcontent.com/pod-product-compliance
Ingram Content Group UK Ltd.
Pitfield, Milton Keynes, MK11 3LW, UK
UKHW041928190726
13854UKWH00004B/1513

9 781291 450989